Why Animals Have Tails

For a free color catalog describing Gareth Stevens' list of high-quality books and multimedia programs, call 1-800-542-2595 (USA) or 1-800-461-9120 (Canada). Gareth Stevens Publishing's Fax: (414) 332-3567.

Library of Congress Cataloging-in-Publication Data available upon request from publisher. Fax: (414) 332-3567 for the attention of the Publishing Records Department.

ISBN 0-8368-2716-3

This North American edition first published in 2000 by
Gareth Stevens Publishing
A World Almanac Education Group Company
330 West Olive Street, Suite 100
Milwaukee, WI 53212 USA

This U.S. edition © 2000 by Gareth Stevens, Inc.
First published as *Ik Heb Een Staart* with an original © 1997
by Mozaïek, an imprint of Uitgeverij Clavis, Hasselt.
Additional end matter © 2000 by Gareth Stevens, Inc.

Text and illustrations: Renne
English translation: Alison Taurel
English text: Dorothy L. Gibbs
Gareth Stevens series editor: Dorothy L. Gibbs
Editorial assistant: Diane Laska-Swanke

Printed in the United States of America

1 2 3 4 5 6 7 8 9 04 03 02 01 00

Why Animals Have Tails

Renne

Gareth Stevens Publishing
A WORLD ALMANAC EDUCATION GROUP COMPANY

Long ago, not all animals looked like the animals we know today. Animals evolved because they needed to adapt to the world around them. Adapting is the reason some animals now have a long neck, a trunk, or large feet.

yellow-billed hornbills

leopard

giraffe

African elephant

European rollers

green mamba

butterfly

springboks

elephant shrews

African rock python

gerenuk

A domestic dog probably developed from a w
This dog does not look like a wolf, but it still h
the same kinds of features.

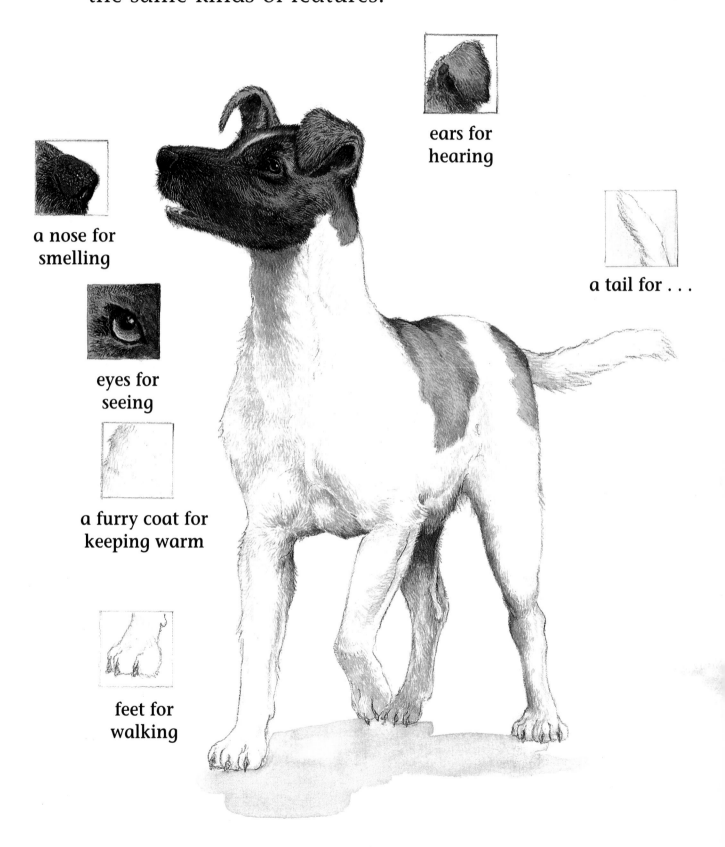

ears for
hearing

a nose for
smelling

a tail for . . .

eyes for
seeing

a furry coat for
keeping warm

feet for
walking

Why does the dog have a tail?

Why do all of these animals have tails?

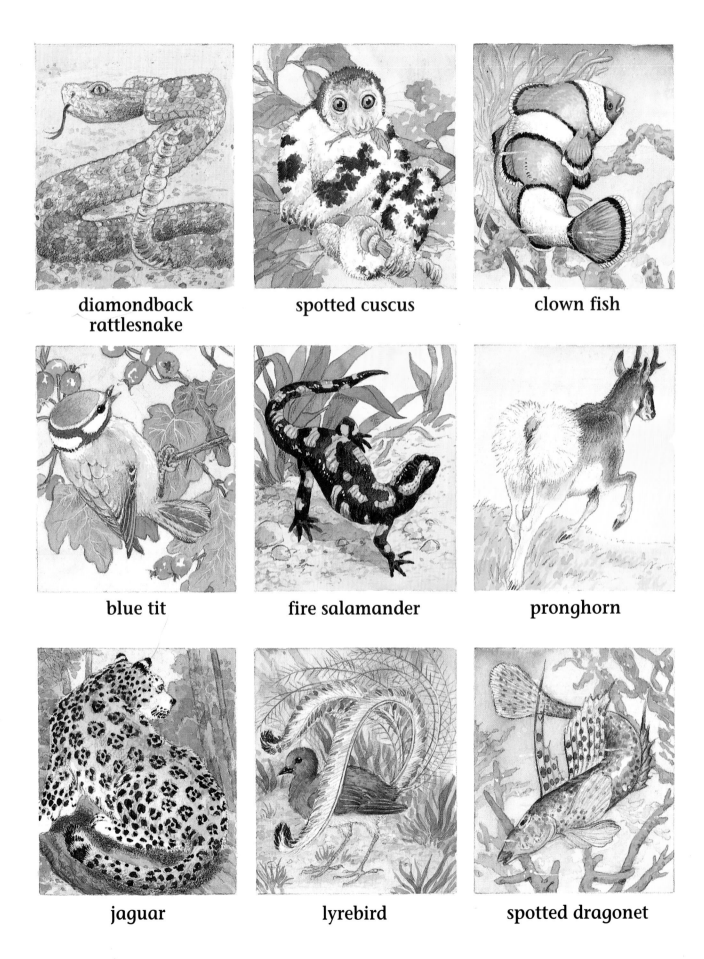

diamondback
rattlesnake

spotted cuscus

clown fish

blue tit

fire salamander

pronghorn

jaguar

lyrebird

spotted dragonet

What is a tail for?

dugong

chinstrap penguins

ring-tailed lemur

green woodpecker

alpine newt

giraffe

gila monster

spiny lobster

blue shark

Dogs, wolves, and many other animals communicate, or "talk," with the help of their tails.

Want to fight?

I'm the boss!

I will obey.

I'm not interested.

I'm staying right where I am.

I'm in a good mood.

Special markings on an animal's fur are also a form of communication. They help animals of the same species recognize each other.

ring-tailed lemurs

genet

red pandas

raccoons

coatis

Some animals use their tails
to sound an alarm.

The tail markings of a frightened
deer signal the direction in
which it is running away.

white-tailed deer

cougar

beaver

A beaver warns that danger
is near by slapping its
tail on the water.

rattlesnake

A rattlesnake keeps
intruders away with its rattle.

These birds have magnificent tails, which they use for finding a mate.

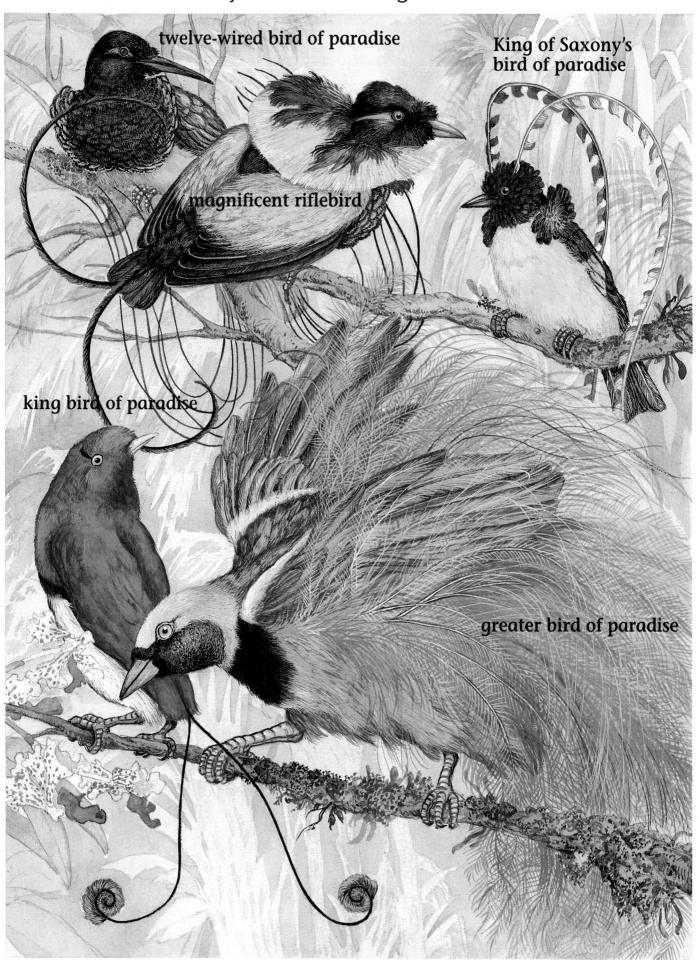

twelve-wired bird of paradise

King of Saxony's bird of paradise

magnificent riflebird

king bird of paradise

greater bird of paradise

More importantly, however, birds use their tails to help them move around. Their tails help birds determine their direction of flight, stop when they land, and balance on branches.

bluethroat

Tails help other kinds of animals move around — or sit still — too.

The animals with these tails can attach themselves to the branches of trees. To which animals do these tails belong?

Others have tails that help them balance as they sit on thin twigs or leap from branch to branch.

10. red uakari
11. woolly ape
12. harvest mouse
13. tarsier
14. tree porcupine
15. dormouse
16. cuscus
17. ruffed lemur
18. rat snake

Many animals live in trees. Some have prehensile tails that help them hang on to branches.

1. spider monkey
2. green tree python
3. green anole
4. aye-aye
5. marmoset
6. pangolin
7. golden lion tamarins
8. colobus
9. tree kangaroo

red howler monkey

kinkajou

tamandua

green tree
monitor

boa constrictor

honey possum

19. tree gecko
20. emerald tree boa
21. chameleon
22. wildcat
23. bare-tailed woolly opossum

Animals that fly from tree to tree, such as birds and flying squirrels, determine their direction of flight with their tails.

The path a flying squirrel takes to get from one tree to another is guided by the squirrel's tail.

sugar glider

red squirrel

pine marten

cheetah

Tails help these animals keep their balance and change direction quickly.

red fox

frilled dragon

Some animals use their tails in a very different way — to keep themselves standing upright!

green woodpecker

gray kangaroos

meerkats

emperor penguins

Sea animals of all kinds have strong tails that help them swim.

1. whale shark
2. pilot fish
3. great white shark
4. brown meagre
5. bluefin tuna
6. crocodile
7. marine iguana
8. sea otter
9. sea snake
10. manatee
11. lobster
12. Norway lobster
13. opah
14. pandora
15. sperm whale
16. narwhal
17. oarfish
18. swordfish
19. balloon fish
20. spiny lobsters

21. conger eel
22. mackerel
23. damselfish

 fish

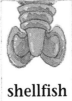 whale

 shellfish

 reptile

mammal

Sea mammals have a lot of power in their tails!

They do many different things with the help of their tails.

Dolphins and flying fish
leap with their tails.

A southern
right whale defends
itself with its tail.

The tails of killer whales
help them swim very fast.

A tail is also useful for getting rid of pests and predators.

Horses, giraffes, lions, and cows have built-in flyswatters.

A red squirrel uses its tail as a blanket when it's cold.

A pangolin uses its tail as a prickly shield to keep predators away.

The tails of some reptiles often save their lives.

When a predator thinks it is biting the head of a northern leaf-tailed gecko, it might actually be biting the gecko's tail.

When a predator catches a slowworm by the tail, the tail breaks off, and the slowworm gets away.

A cyclura iguana, or ground iguana, scares off its predators by whipping its tail around wildly.

When a knob-tailed gecko can't find anything to eat, it can survive on the reserves of fat in its tail.

Other animals keep reserves of fat in their bodies, too —
but not always in their tails.

Camels and
dromedaries keep their
reserves in their humps.

Beavers, fat-tailed dunnarts, and greater dwarf lemurs keep their
reserves of fat in their tails.

Of all the animals in the world, the opossum probably makes the most use of its tail.

North American opossums

On the other hand, there are animals, such as the capybara, that have no tail at all. Even though tails are very useful, animals without tails have adapted to the world around them in other ways.
They do not need tails to survive.

capybara

All of these animals get along just fine without tails!

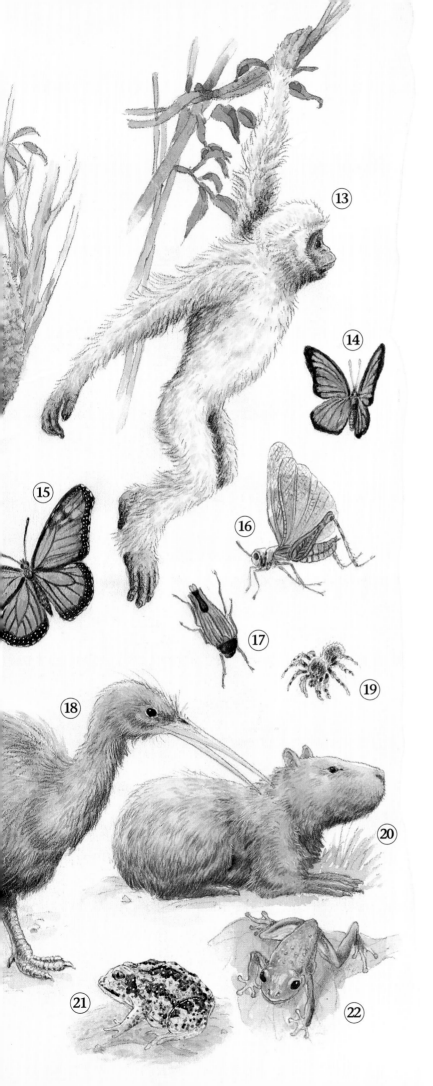

1. gorilla

2. orangutan

3. koala

4. chimpanzees

5. slender loris

6. mosquito

7. agouti

8. sea urchin

9. guinea pig

10. rock hyrax

11. pilgrim scallop

12. starfish

13. white-cheeked gibbon

14. blue morpho butterfly

15. monarch butterfly

16. grasshopper

17. black-tipped wood borer

18. brown kiwi

19. tarantula

20. capybara

21. spadefoot toad

22. tree frog

Glossary

adapt: to change or adjust behavior or appearance to meet the existing conditions of an environment. An animal that does not adapt to its environment might not survive.

alarm: (n) a signal, such as a sound or a movement, that warns others of danger.

balance: to hold steady in a position that keeps weight evenly distributed on all sides.

communicate: to "talk;" to pass on or exchange information with words or unspoken signs or signals.

defends: stands up for or protects, often using physical force or a weapon, something that is in danger of being taken or harmed.

domestic: tamed; not wild; living peacefully and cooperatively among humans; related to home or family. Pets, such as dogs and cats, and farm animals, such as horses, cows, and chickens, are domestic animals.

environments: habitats; areas or regions with certain characteristic climates, sources of food and water, types of animal and plant life, and amounts of human development, all of which define the conditions in which animals and plants in those areas must live.

evolution: the gradual development of animals and plants from earlier forms to present forms, through a series of changes over many years, and from generation to generation.

flyswatters: implements, or tools, that have a flat piece of plastic or wire mesh attached to a long handle and are used to swat at or hit flying insect pests.

intruders: people or things that come into a place or a situation without permission or an invitation, often pushing or forcing their way in and meaning to cause trouble or to harm someone or something.

mammals: animals with backbones and hair or fur on their bodies. Female mammals usually give birth to live young and feed them with milk from their bodies.

pests: small animals, such as insects, that are annoying or cause trouble.

prehensile: able to grasp or hold onto something by wrapping around it. Animals with prehensile tails often wrap them around tree branches both to hang on and to keep their balance.

reptiles: air-breathing animals that have backbones and, usually, slimy or scaly skin. Reptiles move around by sliding on their bellies, like snakes, or crawling on very short legs, like lizards.

reserves: supplies that are stored, held back, or set aside to be used later or in a time of special need.

species: a certain group of animals that look and act very much alike and can mate with each other.

upright: straight, or erect, in a vertical, or up and down, position.

More Books to Read

Animal Communication. Naturebooks (series). Janet McDonnell (Child's World)

Animals in Motion: How Animals Swim, Jump, Slither, and Glide. Pamela Hickman (Kids Can Press)

AnimalTalk. TableTalk Conversation Cards (series). J. J. Stupp (TableTalk/The Booksource)

Dogs: The Wolf Within. Understanding Animals (series). Dorothy Hinshaw Patent (Carolrhoda Books)

How Animals Move. Animal Survival (series). Michel Barré (Gareth Stevens)

Lemurs, Lorises, and Other Lower Primates. Patricia A. Fink Martin (Children's Press)

Tails That Talk and Fly. Up Close (series). Diane Swanson (Douglas & McIntyre, Ltd.)

What on Earth Is a Capybara? What on Earth (series). Edward R. Ricciuti (Blackbirch Marketing)

Videos

Animal Acrobats. Animal Talk. Henry's Amazing Animals (series). (Dorling Kindersley)

Animal Life for Children: All about Animal Adaptations. (Schlessinger)

Hot Dogs and Cool Cats. (National Geographic Kids Video)

How Animals Move. How Animals Talk. Tree Living Animals. Animals in Action (series). (Kodak Video)

Monkeys. First Time Science (series). (Troll Associates)

Wolves. The Friendly Forest Club (series). (Big Kids Productions)

Web Sites

Cetacea Behavior. *nmml.afsc.noaa.gov/education/ cetaceans/cetaceabeh.htm*

Dinosaur Tails. *www.enchantedlearning.com/subjects/ dinosaurs/anatomy/tail.shtml*

Eye on Tails. *www.unicornink.com/ ttf/tails.html*

Pure Illusion Arabians and Cross-breeds. Evolution of the Horse Presentation. *www.facethemusic.org/ evolution.html*

To find additional Web sites, use a reliable search engine with one or more of the following keywords: *animal behavior, animal communication, beaver, dog, evolution, fluke, kinkajou, monkey, motion, prehensile tail, tail,* and *whale.*

Index